A ROOM FOR DAVID

. . . SPIRITUAL HEALER

David Sampson

A ROOM FOR DAVID
... SPIRITUAL HEALER

By
HELEN VINALL

WITH SPECIFIC EXPLANATIONS
AND FINAL CHAPTER
BY
DAVID SAMPSON

L. N. FOWLER & CO. LTD.
1201 HIGH ROAD,
CHADWELL HEATH,
ROMFORD, ESSEX RM6 4DH

ISBN 0 85243 377 8

Photoset by
PEARL GRAPHIC LIMITED LEYTONSTONE E10

PRINTED AND BOUND IN GREAT BRITAIN BY
A WHEATON & CO LTD EXETER

DEDICATION

To David Sampson, my very good friend.

THANKS

Sincere ones. To everyone who has
helped in the making of this tribute
to Spiritual Healing. To all the
patients who have contributed case
histories and confidence, to Ann
Moody, who offered to type the
manuscript before she'd even seen my
handwriting, and has never actually
said she regretted it! To Brian
Stockwell, who has vetted and advised
when the writing has flourished,and
prodded persistently, aided by his
wife, Jenny, when it has flagged.
To Malcolm Williams, who offered to
"do" the cover for us, and took our
vague request for "a sort of cottage,
with light coming from the Healing Room"
and turned it, most effectively, into
just that. To these, and to the
hundreds of patients who have wished
the venture well, my thanks.

AUTHOR'S NOTE

This is a very small book about a very large subject. It does not set out to analyse, justify or probe deeply into Spiritual Healing. This power, like the God from whom it flows, just IS and this little book is just an account of what has been happening – to David Sampson, and me, and thousands of patients – throughtout the last five years, in my little home.

CHAPTERS

CHAPTER 1

HOW I MET DAVID

In July 1979 my right wrist was very painful and stiff, so stiff that I could not turn a tap or undo a screwtop jar. The knuckles on that hand were also very red and swollen, making it difficult for me to cope with many everyday jobs, including writing. "You ought to let David see that wrist" said my friend "I'm sure that he could help". "And who", I asked "is David, and how can he help?" "He's a Spiritual Healer" she replied "He's at my house every Thursday evening from 7.30 p.m. and if you'll come along you can see for yourself what he can do".

Now my friend, Ella, was no fool. I respected her judgement. For many years we had worked together at the local Primary School, where she was a teacher and I was the secretary. We had retired within a couple of years of each other, we had been widowed within a few months of each other, after we had each known the helpless misery of watching a husband slowly dying. In addition she had suffered two sub-arachnoid haemorrhages, and she knew the score. I had seen her in such misery that her face was a mask, eyes shuttered against the seething pain behind them. Drugs afforded little relief, and her future must have looked bleak indeed. But she was a wonderful person, loving and caring towards others, and she hid her suffering as much as possible. I had to admit, however, that she certainly seemed much better lately, less strained. Indeed, when I really thought about it, she *must* be better, for she could certainly not have coped with a roomful of people, chattering through a whole evening, a few months ago. So – if Ella thought that David could help me, there must be something very special about this Spiritual Healing that he was dispensing, and I would be a fool not to avail myself of it. But I didn't. Not for another six weeks anyway, by which time the pain in my wrist was much worse, and I was fast becoming ambidextrous. I was also learning a lot more about David Sampson.

Charlie, our window cleaner was the first person to sing his praises to me. Charlie's back had been so weak when he first met David that he could not stand. His friend told me that he had been to Charlie's house on Christmas Day and found him draped over the back of a chair – his Christmas dinner on the seat – the only way he could join his family at the table and eat his meal with them. He had had a bad back for sixteen years – the lumbar nerve was damaged. He had endured traction – had been in full plaster, and had treatment from osteopaths, but nothing had helped. It took just six treatments by Spiritual Healing to restore that back to normality. That was in 1979. In 1980-81 Charlie and his son dug out nearly 200 tons of clay, manually, to make a swimming pool in a garden where access for the necessary earth-moving machinery was impossible. The whole family, including pets, now come to David as soon as they have a health problem.

His friend, Dennis, had a similar tale to tell. He too, was crippled by a back injury that was not helped by any of the usual treatments, and he was in a state of deep depression over his inability to work when he heard about Spiritual Healing. Both the injury and the depression yielded to Healing and he was able to return to a full and active life. Many of his colleagues, impressed by the change in him, have also been to David for healing for a variety of complaints.

I began to feel that I was being steered firmly in the direction of Mr. Sampson, and since I have long believed that nothing happens by chance, I finally gave in, and went to see him.

The atmosphere in Ella's house was warm and friendly and there was a lot of laughter. About half a dozen people were waiting to see David, who was in the dining room. When it was my turn to go in, Ella introduced us, saying "This is Helen, and she's brought her wrist". "Good" said David "that should make it easier – come and sit down". And that was my first meeting with David Sampson – a meeting that was to lead to a new and wonderful way of life for me, that was to bring me into contact with hundreds of sick, weary, sometimes desperate, people, whose lives would be changed and enriched by Spiritual Healing.

The first impression I had when David took my wrist between his hands was of warmth and strength flowing into it, then after two or three minutes he went behind me and put his hands on my shoulders, saying "You have an old injury here that is causing you trouble". His hands were vibrating, and again warmth came through them, then suddenly he put both hands over my left eye, and they were very cold "What is the matter with your eye?" he asked "I have a strong signal that something is wrong here". I was so amazed that I could not answer coherently, but in fact I had recently attended the hospital because I had had white flashes, like tracer shells, making a moving bead curtain down the front of my left eye. After exhaustive tests they had been unable to find the cause, and as it didn't happen all the time, though most uncomfortable when it did, I wasn't unduly worried. Whatever it was, it has never happened since. After three visits my wrist was completely freed, and has remained so. The shoulders took considerably longer, but then, it was twenty years since I had tried to pull a little tree out of the garden not realising that that particular little tree was like an iceberg – only the top third was visible. My tug-of-war with the roots ended in a jerk that left me feeling that my spine had been kicked upwards into my cranium. Over the years the various pains and discomforts had settled into a steady ache across the shoulders – much valued by my family as a weather forecast. Many a drenching was avoided by a correct evaluation of the extent of Mother's twinges! However, anyone who has endured a dreary backache for many years knows that it isn't really funny, and I found it almost impossible to believe that it had really gone when it was finally banished by the power that came through David's hands. Not only were my shoulders eased, but a slight curvature that I had had since childhood was corrected, and a troublesome and painful hip joint troubles me no longer.

Ella had, for some time, been considering selling her house and moving to Cleveland to be near her sister, but had been unable to face the worry of making all the arrangements. Now, however, she was feeling so well that she was confident that she could deal with the necessary business, and the wheels were set in motion.

My children had married and moved away by then, and my husband had died the previous year after a long illness that had necessitated constant nursing. I was rather like a ship without a rudder at that time, and longing desperately for something to give some meaning to my life, so when Ella told me, at the end of October, that her house was sold, and asked if I could possibly find room for David I was delighted to offer him the use of my home as a centre for healing. Thus began a working partnership that has lasted over five years, and that has given my life depth and richness, and made me almost blasé about miracles.

CHAPTER 2

HOW DAVID MET HEALING

David Loxdale Sampson was born in South Africa on Armistice Day, 11th November, 1930. His mother, from whom he got his middle name, was English, a Londoner, but her family came originally from Shrewsbury, where various of her ancestors had held office as Mayors, and as Under Sheriffs of Shropshire during the 18th and 19th Centuries.

His father was South African, but his great-grandfather hailed from Devon. David was the youngest of four children, having one brother and two sisters. His brother, John, was also born on Armistice Day, and when David arrived he was presented to John, aged 4, as a birthday present – a gift which might have been received with mixed feelings. Some youngsters might have preferred a puppy or a train set. Not so John. He was, I am assured by David, delighted to have a baby brother for his very own, and indeed they have had a wonderful relationship throughout their lives.

Theirs was a loving, caring family, giving each other support and consideration at all times. They were not rich, father was an accountant, and a lay preacher, loved and respected as a man who gave time and help whenever it was needed. He died when David was ten, having retired a few years before to start a flower farm near Pietermaritzburg –a lifelong ambition realised. John then became the man of the family, and his influence was very important in David's development. They had to give up the market garden and move into Pietermaritzburg, where they continued their education. John was a brilliant student, embarking at sixteen on a five year course that was to make him a Char-

tered Accountant a few weeks after his twenty first birthday –
nearly two of those years having been spent in wartime
service in the Navy! David is very proud of John, who is a
fine musician and inventive engineer as well, but he never
made his young brother feel inadequate because he was not
equally gifted, – for this David is very grateful. His sisters
also he describes as "marvellous" and he considers himself
very lucky to have been born into such a happy Christian family.

His English mother had instilled into him a great love for
her distant home, and when he was twenty one David
decided to spend his "birthday money" on a trip to England
to see the places he had heard so much about. March 1952
saw him sailing up Southampton Water to begin what he
thought would be a two to three month visit to this country,
a visit that has lasted, so far, thirty three years. He must have
been the ideal tourist, for he revelled in everything he saw.
London fully lived up to his mother's enthusiastic descrip-
tions, and he loved it! When money began to run out he
took a temporary job as a clerk in the works department of
Blue Star Garages in Chelsea. The job proved to be as temporary as his holiday. Instead of the three weeks for which
he was engaged, he stayed twenty four and a half years and
became Branch Manager of the company's Chelsea business.

When David came to Britain he had a health problem.
Since childhood his head and neck had inclined to the right.
His neck was often swollen, and he suffered severe migraine
attacks. These were frequent enough to prove a setback to
his advancement in business and he decided to seek the very
best medical advice available. His own G.P. had sent him
for X-Rays, as a result of which he was told that a malformation of the spine was the cause of the trouble and nothing
could be done about it.

Through being based in Chelsea he knew many well-
known stage people, and top-ranking doctors. He asked six
doctors who they would go to if they had his problem. Four

of the six suggested a consultant at St. Georges Hospital. David found him most helpful and concerned, but when he again went for X-Rays the same verdict was arrived at. The tilt of the head and resultant migraine was caused by a malformation of the spine. He had already tested various drugs, some of which made him very sick, and none of which helped. An operation was deemed inadvisable, the only help offered was painkillers, but a course of exercises to control and relax muscles and thus to relieve tension was recommended. These took place at the Anderson Clinic in Kensington, and they certainly helped to reduce the number of migraine attacks. They were however, very expensive, and David found it difficult to afford the very frequent sessions that were needed.

Among the well known stage folk who used the garage in Chelsea was Katie Boyle. She had received healing from Ted Fricker of Wyndham Place, with dramatic results, and for two years had been trying to persuade David, and his colleague Jean Johnston, to go to the healer for help. So far they had refused, but the day came when Jean, desperate with pain in her back, pain that consistently defied any form of treatment or medication, finally rang for an appointment and, amazingly, was able to be seen at once. She was rather disappointed to be met by Mrs. Fricker, who explained that she too was a healer and helped her husband at particularly busy times, or when he had to be elsewhere. Jean received immediate relief, so much so that when she returned to the office, she proceeded to demonstrate the then popular "twist". David had to take notice of this, after all, he had worked with Jean for many years, and had often seen her in great pain. Now she was moving freely, quite without pain, after a treatment lasting only a few minutes. She had to return a couple of weeks later for her second appointment, and this time she saw Mr. Fricker, and, realising that something almost miraculous was happening to her, she made an appointment for David. He went, somewhat reluctantly, and apologised for wasting Mr. Fricker's time, explaining that he had a malformed spine and that nothing could be done about it. Ted Fricker was obviously unimpressed by this diagnosis, remarking amiably that it was "a lot of blooming nonsense" – the top disc was out and it wouldn't show in an X-Ray anyway. To this he added his belief that David had fallen on his head when he was a child. As he was pondering this statement David was conscious of warmth coming from the healer's hands, and in a few minutes he could move his neck with ease.

Next day he had a really vicious migraine – so severe that he would have swallowed every pill in the bathroom cabinet if he could have staggered along there to get them. By the evening it had gone, and he never had another. Later he was healed of a heart condition and of very painful haemorrhoids, but by now he knew that it was not only a physical change that he was undergoing. He felt that he was changing spiritually as well. He was very shaken by what had happened to him, and he would lie awake at night wondering just what this power was that had healed him. Ted Fricker claimed that it was the work of God, and it seemed to David that it must be so. He had found Mr. Fricker to be a simple, direct person, and had warmed to him from his first visit. He wanted more information about this healing and he began to read books, some of which the healer lent him, and both he and Jean started taking people along for healing. However busy he was – and people came to him from all over the world – Ted always managed to fit in the patients that David and Jean brought. All were helped, most were healed, some quite dramatically, and David got to know the Fricker family very well.

He was however, very puzzled by the idea that he had fallen on his head when he was a child, as he had no recollection of such a fall, nor had his family ever mentioned it. Then he remembered an accident that had nearly ended in tragedy, and which would make Mr. Fricker's statement seem accurate. As a youngster he had fallen from a tree and was knocked out. His cousin, who was close by, watering the garden, saw that David was not moving, so turned the hose pipe directly to his face in the belief that cold water poured on to an unconscious being would restore life immediately. It nearly did the opposite by half-drowning David, who received the full flow in his mouth and needed artificial respiration to regain his breathing. He thereby gained a certain notoriety in the family as the only person who had nearly drowned miles away from any river, lake or sea, but he never realised that that must have been the time when his neck was injured.

About ten years after David was healed, the firm for whom he worked sold out to an American oil company, and most of the staff decided to leave. All of the office staff were "Frickerites" by this time, and Ted gave a farewell dinner party for them at a South Kensington restaurant. During the evening he took David aside and told him that he, too, had the gift of healing, and that he must use it. David found this difficult to believe but during the next few weeks he went along to the surgery and helped with some of the patients. He himself felt nothing during these sessions, and was doubtful whether he was actually giving healing, but Mr. Fricker always took over from him, for which he was very grateful.

Then, one evening he arrived home to find that his wife, Marjorie, had fallen from a kitchen stool and injured her leg. It was so swollen and painful that she could not stand, but when David said that he would phone their doctor she suggested that he should give her healing instead, which he did, and after a short while the swelling subsided, the pain went, and she was quite alright again.

Shortly after that they decided to move to Bexhill, in Sussex. A friend offered them the use of a flat whilst they looked for a suitable property, and, on their first night there, David awoke to hear their sixteen year old son gasping for breath. He went in to find the lad looking very ill indeed, in the throes of an asthma attack, unable to get any air. It was a frightening situation, for they knew nobody in

Bexhill, certainly no doctors, and once again it was Marjorie who suggested that David should give healing. He did so, with some misgiving, but in a few minutes the boy became calmer, was able to breathe easily and soon fell asleep. He has not had an attack since. This convinced David that he must use this God-given gift to help people. They bought a house in Little Common and he began to give healing to friends and colleagues, who, in turn recommended *their* friends and colleagues. It was in this way that he was introduced to Una Lyons, who had been going to Ted Fricker for sometime with eye trouble, but had not been helped. For this reason David was rather dubious about offering healing, but there was a dramatic improvement the very first time he did so, and he felt that he had definitely been guided to Una, that this was a special healing. It further strengthened his belief that this gift was to be taken very seriously, as it was obviously going to be a very important part of his life in future.

CHAPTER 3

"LITTLE PATCHES"

When David first started healing at my home he was work-ing by day, and seeing people on one evening each week. He made no charge. Between ten and eighteen was the usual number; they waited in my sitting room, received healing in the dining room, and had a cup of tea and a lot of laughs as a bonus. But after nearly two years of widowhood, I was find-ing that the upkeep of my house and garden, which I loved, was too much for me, so when a friend who lived nearly opposite me, decided to sell her cottage, I asked her to give me first refusal. She agreed, saying "But I don't think you'll like it, Helen, because there's not much garden, only these two little patches". The "little patches" were a small paved area at the back, bordered by a ditch and a hedge, and a flowerbed under the front window. I bought it and called it "Little Patches". There is only a large sitting room and a kitchen downstairs, but as we only had a few patients, on one evening a week, and as David declared that it was "a cracking little place, and the atmosphere was marvellous, and it's the healing that matters and not the setting", that was adequate. People waited in the sitting room and were healed in the kitchen. They still are, but nowadays there are well over a hundred of them each week!

Towards the end of 1980 David began to feel that healing was coming between him and his work, and he had to make a big decision. Where did his future lie? He and his wife spent many hours talking and seeking guidance, and finally, in January 1981 he gave up a very lucrative job to devote his life to Spiritual Healing. I remember saying "This is like going over Beachy Head without a parachute, David, are you absolutely sure it's the right thing to do? What will you

23

live on?" "I have some savings" he replied "I know that I have to do it – and I know also that I shall be looked after". His faith has been justified. He does now ask that those who can should leave a modest fee, but stresses that, if this a problem, patients should speak to him about it. I have no idea who pays, or how much, and I don't really think David does either. There is a bowl in the room where healing takes place, and at the end of the day there is money in it. That's all. To begin with, David saw patients on Wednesday afternoon and evenings, but soon the morning was taken over as well. Then came the glorious day when we had fifty three patients – seventeen of them at one time! Every seat was taken and they were sitting on the stairs. Some waited nearly three hours to see David, but everyone was happy. The atmosphere was wonderful, but it was obvious that this must not happen regularly – three hours is a large slab out of anyone's day! So we spread to Thursdays, soon added Mondays, and began to operate an appointment system. An appointment system that is, I firmly believe, unique. No urgent case is ever refused, so we often have two – sometimes three – names on the same line, which necessitates there being at least 90 minutes in some hours, which there aren't, yet everybody gets seen, so there must be! If things get really sticky then someone always phones to cancel their appointment – just where we need another few minutes. I sometimes feel that there must be someone "Up there" who can't abide chaotic appointment books, and so proceeds, with enviable efficiency, to clear the channels. I send him/ her my salaams!

I never dreamed when I bought my little cottage, that this would happen. Little did I think, as I watched my carpet being laid, that within a year over two hundred strange (some *very* strange) feet would tramp across it each week, and, as I saw my already mature armchairs being manoeuvred through the tiny entrance lobby, I had no premonition that they would soon play host to some 5,200 assorted posteriors per annum. But I love it! I really do. I have always liked people. I thoroughly enjoyed my twenty six years as a school secretary, coping with small people, and I often find a parallel between a somewhat apprehensive new patient who has come to see David and an equally apprehensive parent who had come to see the Headmaster. There is the same feeling of "What have I let myself in for?". Laughter is the best release here, and as David and I share an identical sense of humour, he often caps my remarks and the patient goes through to him on a wave of laughter, relaxed and receptive to healing.

As well as liking people, I also like craftwork. I make soft toys, music boxes, do some embroidery and beadwork and a bit of woodcarving. I also make wine. There is usually a half-made toy or piece of other craftwork lying around, and it makes a talking point. Often I find a fellow enthusiast, and we exchange ideas and patterns, but woe betide the poor benighted soul who mentions, casually, that she has always thought that, one day, she would like to make a rag doll – or teddy – or whatever I'm engaged upon. Without knowing quite how it happened she discovers that this *is* that "one day" and she finds herself going home with patterns, materials, stuffing and, hopefully, enthusiasm. Quite a number of beds in Sussex sprouted patchwork quilts when I was making mine, and it was at that time that our male patients took to wearing open-neck shirts after I admired the material of their ties, pleading that I only needed a two-inch square to complete *the* most perfect colour scheme. I never got it.

Wine is a notorious loosener of tongues, but when it is safely bubbling away in a demijohn in the corner of my room, that can only be a good thing. The most unexpected people turn out to be winemakers, and recipes and tips are exchanged, enthusiasm is generated, and, by the time their turn comes, they and our incipient toy makers are completely relaxed and David's warm welcome starts the healing process.

Since David was told, in 1975, that he had this gift, hun-

dreds of people have received healing through his hands
and hundreds more through Absent (or Distant) Healing.
Not everyone is completely healed; most are – some within
a few minutes, some after several visits, others after months
–even years, but all are helped in some degree. Many are
kept free of pain, others acquire a serenity that helps them
bear their burden more easily. I never ask patients what is
wrong with them, that is between them and David, and we
seldom discuss patients. That is the way they want it, a one-
to-one relationship with their healer, but sometimes someone will say "Until I came here I never thought I'd ever be
free of backache (or migraine – or eczema – or sinus trouble
etc.) again", and then the floodgates are opened, everyone
talks about their healing, and I realise what a load of unhappiness, and sheer drudgery of pain these people coped with
before meeting David. They come from all over South East
England, and from every income level. One thing they have
in common, conventional medicine has not worked for
them. They have heard about David from others who have
received healing, and so they come, often in desperation, to
see if he can help them.

"Little Patches" is a humble setting for a gift administered
with humility by our healer, and when he is here, the love
that flows through my little home is so strong as to be almost
tangible.

On "Healing Days" the front door is always open. Old
hands come in and choose a chair to suit their backaches, if
any, to make themselves happily at home. New patients are
often apprehensive, they are not at all sure what is going to
happen to them. In fact one lass confessed that she didn't
know if David would be dressed in a "Jesus robe", a crimson
lined cloak and top hat, or have a bone through his nose!
(Actually he dresses very conventionally and heals "in his
shirtsleeves").

One man, a real cockney, was so scared on his first visit
that he was visibly shaking whilst he waited, and David said
he was fairly vibrating during the healing session – he

seemed to think he wasn't eligible because "I don't go to church nor nuffink". He had a really hideous leg, a varicose ulcer that was almost gangrenous, but which is now almost healed, only a tiny scab remaining.

He is a constant source of enjoyment to us all with his rhyming slang. He threw David completely the first time he asked if he could do anything "Abaht me strawberry tart" – his heart. Having mastered that one, we didn't take quite so long to unravel "I reckon I'm okay now except for me British Rail". Now, David figured that B.R. deals with trains, which rhymes with brains, and we were home and dry! In fact David is now so proficient in this lovely language that he didn't hesitate to commiserate when Dougie phoned to say "Shan't be dahn Monday Dave, some tea-leaf's half-inched me wheels". It's no joke having your car stolen, but fortunately the "tea leaf" was stupid enough to try doing seventy through a built up area. This misdemeanour was observed by an off-duty, but still alert policeman, and Dougie now has his wheels back. He still "doesn't go to church nor nuffink", but he's a wonderful person, generous, always ready to help anyone, and whole-hearted in his belief in Spiritual Healing. He doesn't understand it – he just knows, in his heart, that it works.

Not everyone, thank goodness, is as fearful as Doug was on his first visit, but people do sometimes come with some rather odd ideas about what happens. Well-meaning friends, who know nothing about Spiritual Healing, may have voiced dark suspicions about "getting undressed", not realising that healing works through any number of layers, including your "thermals". Not a garment need be shed, not even a top coat, if the patient wants to stay muffled, indeed I have known at least three backs that have been healed through plaster casts.

One girl, having been warned by her nearest and dearest "Whatever you do, don't meet his eyes or he'll hypnotise you" charged through the room with lowered head, and sat looking fixedly at the floor during healing – a somewhat wasted effort since David always heals from behind or beside his patient, unless feet or legs are involved. She laughs about it now, and "laughs" is the important word in that sentence for she was a desperately unhappy lass when she first came to "Little Patches". Severe back pain, and dread of an impending operation had made her short-tempered and difficult to work with. She asked for the operation to be deferred, and when she went later to the specialist to see if it was still necessary he found that her back was completely healed. Not only that, she was now a relaxed and happy person, very popular with her colleagues. It is wonderful when that happens, when the mask that pain or stress has formed, cracks and falls away and the real person smiles through. Then the healer's work is truly done, the patient is "whole" again. In this particular case the healing resulted in her taking a renewed interest in the Church, and she, and her mother, also one of David's patients, were recently baptized.

CHAPTER 4

HEALING IS FOR WHAT NEEDS HEALING

People often phone to ask "Can he help with my arthritis" – or cancer – or psoriasis – or depression – or any of a dozen other complaints. The answer is that healing is for whatever needs healing, but David does not know, until he puts his hands on the patient, just what help will be given. Sometimes the cure is instantaneous, as with the girl who sneezed so violently that she tore a muscle in her back and put a disc out. On her way to collect a prescription for painkillers she called on a friend who was just setting out to see David. He brought her along, and I watched her get slowly out of the car and walk with difficulty into the house. A few minutes later I watched her emerge, looking quite bewildered, from her healing session, repeating over and over "I can't believe it" – the words that I hear *so* often – as she realised that she was completely free of pain, and could walk normally. Every healing is wonderful, but these are the ones that, figuratively speaking, grab you by the lapels and shake you, making you realise the potency of this wonderful Spiritual force.

There was one particular afternoon when there was a positive plethora of "lapel-shaking". About half a dozen patients were there, and we were discussing a newspaper article that someone had brought in. It was completely dismissive of all types of alternative medicine, osteopathy, homeopathy, acupuncture, faith healing – the lot. When I had read it I said "This makes me want to weep" whereupon Margaret said "Then I think this is the time for me to tell you what the Consultant said to me yesterday. My condition is still stable, he is completely baffled, he has never met this situation before, and he just hasn't any advice or treatment to offer me". And she sat there beaming at us, this young teacher, mother of two youngsters, who was told in 1983 that she had leukaemia, and could not expect to live more than two years. The drug she was given had such vicious side-effects that it was stopped after a few months and there was no other that could be offered. Meanwhile she had met David, and had been receiving healing twice weekly, and, apart from a couple of "hiccups" when she had been over-doing things, had made slow but steady progress. Her last two blood tests had shown the balance restored, and yet the disease had not been treated medically, for months. No wonder she was smiling.

When she had finished talking and we had all rejoiced with her, a quiet voice said – "Now I'll tell you what the neurologist told me yesterday". This was David W, who has been taking drugs for twenty years following "a couple of blackouts" in 1963. At first the dosage was small but in 1974, when he was 44, he had a full epileptic attack and it was discovered that he had a benign brain tumour. This meant the end of his career, as he was put on a total of 15 pills per day, which turned him into "an introspective zombie", and that's how he was when he first came for healing. He felt an immediate improvement after his first visit, and was able to enjoy a holiday soon after. The improvement continued, he is now fully articulate, loves to discuss books, t.v. programmes etc., and is really good company. His neurologist was much impressed by the difference in him over a six month period and told him to carry on seeing his healer every week, and *their* contribution would be gradual reduction in the drugs prescribed. To hear a doctor was pre-pared to work with a healer in this way was indeed a most hopeful "sign and portent". And there was more to come. David W had been brought along by his neighbour Joan, who had also brought her mother, whom we called Nanny. Nanny had come to spend Christmas with her daughter and had been forced to stay longer than she had intended because of the very bad weather in January, 1985. She had some difficulty in walking and was often in great pain, and this was her fourth visit to David. A few minutes after the three of them had left, Joan came running back to the house, flung her arms round me and cried "Nanny's walking – she suddenly said – Look I'm walking – I'm not crippled anymore" – and she isn't. Isn't it wonderful!" Whereupon she burst into tears, and so did everyone else, and it was *lovely*! Meanwhile, Nanny was refusing to get in the car – back she came to thank David –repeating over and over again – "Isn't it wonderful". David, as ever said "Thank God and bless you", and Nanny was eventually persuaded to get in the car and they departed. A few days later she went back to her own house and celebrated the occasion by running up and down the stairs! It's a wonder the roof stayed on my cottage that day! Joan incidentally, had come originally with a very stiff neck, necessitating the wearing of a neck collar. After the first healing session she could turn her head without pain, and it was this cure that had given David W the impetus to seek healing.

All new patients are given a copy of David's own leaflet on Divine Healing, together with one from the National Federation of Spiritual Healers, of which he is a member, so all are made aware, from the beginning, of the Divine Source of their healing. We do not then discuss the spiritual aspect unless – or, as it is increasingly, *until* – the patient broaches the subject. Then, since the seed is obviously beginning to germinate, we lend books to help feed the growth of awareness, and three or four times a year David holds a meeting to answer questions that he just hasn't time to deal with fully during healing sessions. Like Ted Fricker, David always says – "Don't thank me, thank God for healing", but people want to know more, and these meetings stretch our seating capacity to the full. They are always lively, happy occasions, and we find out so much from the most unexpected people. By the time the tea cups are circulating many misconceptions have been swept away, and many people are rejoicing in the new found comradeship resulting from an open discussion of spiritual matters with folk "like themselves". No abstruse theories are aired, there is just the simple message of God's love expressing itself as healing. In his leaflet "Spiritual Healing. Holistic Way to Health" Don Copland, President of the National Federation of Spiritual Healers, writes of Spiritual Healing "It is the true link between man and God. As there is but one God and healing has been in existence for thousands of years it cannot be claimed to be a personal monopoly of any one religion or faith. The true spiritual healer is a person working irrespective of colour, class or creed. He is a spiritual person in tune with the source of all creation. This linking of the patient to God forms, with the healer, a triangle of attunement that enables the healing energies from a divine source to flow".

In his leaflet David writes "It does not require faith in me, since I have no power, but am purely a channel for this most potent force. This healing is one way in which God proves to us that he exists, and cares".

It has always seemed to me that healing *must* be a joyous thing. After all, most of the people who come to us are "Doctor's Rejects" – they have been told that nothing more can be done, that they must "learn to live with it". But, when God takes over where the Doctor had to leave off, nothing is impossible. Backs can straighten, skins can clear, vision can return, phobias can be banished. The important word is CAN. It does not always happen. Spiritual Healing is "whole" healing, and, to quote Don Copland again "Healing cannot interfere with divine law, nor the free will that we have been granted by God. The choice is ours whether we want to be healed or not". The patient must truly *wish* to be healed. The mere fact that someone has come to a healer would surely imply that the wish was there, but think – how many people do you know whose illnesses are almost their "raison d'être"? At some point their conversation always comes back to what the Doctor said about the unique nature of their complaint, how this was confirmed by the specialist, how the consultant marvelled at their stoicism. Their lives are so little, or so lonely, that their ill-health fills them, and no-one should take that prop away without putting something better in its place. Divine Healing will do this, if the sufferer will accept it. With the physical healing comes a feeling of peace, of freedom from tension, of confidence that all is well. If the patients will then start to look outward instead of inward, and let the love that healed them flow to others, then life will become fuller and more harmonious. People will gravitate to them because of the warmth and kindness they find there, and they will realise that giving comfort to others is more rewarding than soliciting sympathy for oneself. Life will have a new meaning.

Sometimes it is more than a new meaning, sometimes it is virtually a new life that is received through healing. This is especially wonderful when a small child is the patient. We all rejoice with the parents when this happens, when a child who seems doomed to live a very restricted life has the blockage removed, or the limb straightened, or the allergy dealt with, and the future is bright again.

This happened to Helena, a lovely and loving little girl aged three and a half years, who was deemed to be allergic to so many things that her mother was given a list of only ten items of food that would be safe for her. A dreary prospect indeed at three and a half. When David first saw her she was losing weight, listless, with no appetite, and frequently woke during the night with severe abdominal pains. The morning after David's visit a delighted mother phoned to say that her daughter had had a night completely free from pain and had awoken refreshed and hungry. She soon regained her lost weight and within five weeks was eating whatever she wanted, with no ill effects. The difference between the listless, unhappy little girl that David first visited in her home (because she was too ill to be brought to "Little Patches") and the bright-eyed little lass who raced, ponytail swinging, through my sitting room at the end of that five weeks, to hug David's knees and tell him she loved him, was enough to move one to grateful tears. Certainly my throat ached as I watched her. The family moved to Norfolk soon after that but David had a wonderful "thank you" letter from the mother in which she referred to Helena's last visit to the Consultant Paediatrician in Eastbourne "He thought her so much improved that he deemed it unnecessary to refer her to anyone in the Norfolk and Norwich Hospital. As a matter of fact, he and his team were so utterly amazed at Helena's weight increase and her drastic improvement that they asked me what I had done. Well, I sat up straight, looked him straight in the eye, and told him that I was a Christian, and had been to see you. Instead of the sarcastic comment I was expecting he clapped his hands in delight and said how pleased he was, adding that "these people have so much to offer – we are only doctors and we need all the help that we can get". He seemed really thrilled. If only more doctors were as open-minded – the combination of modern medicine and Divine Guidance would be irrestible!

David is wonderful with children. He loves them and they know it, for you can't fool children – or animals. Paul was a tiny "waif", when we first saw him – a year old, and weighing just 13 lbs. He kept regurgitating, his food just would not stay down. (One doctor suggested that he enjoyed regurgitating). He was a lovely little chap with a look of quite disconcerting intelligence in his large, dark blue eyes. As he lay on my carpet with his head cradled on his arm he seemed to be pondering some deep enigmatic problem. "Not in entire forgetfulness" perhaps?

After two visits there was a distinct improvement, and at the third his mother announced proudly that she could now state her small son's weight in stones – albeit only one! It was now obvious that he was continuing to gain weight steadily, and he only needed to come twice more. His mother wrote "At last he's become the happy little boy we were waiting for". Another cause for rejoicing.

CHAPTER 5

QUESTIONS AND ANSWERS

Two or three times a year David has a meeting at "Little Patches" at which he answers the patients' questions on healing – questions which he just hasn't time to deal with fully during healing sessions. We have about fifteen people here each time, and there is always a waiting list of folk wanting to come along.

Most of our patients come to David simply because they need help that orthodox medicine has not been able to give. Their need, at that time, is purely physical – relief from pain, or problem, and their attitude is often that Spiritual Healing is a last resort, or that "it can't do any harm to give it a try". Everyone is given the National Federation of Spiritual Healing leaflet "Holistic Way to Health" and David's own leaflet "Divine Healing". Some are obviously comforted to see that the word "God" appears naturally and frequently in both, others are obviously uncomfortable for the same reason. The latter are often anxious to know what happens during healing, and ask me what they should do, or what they should think about, when they are receiving healing. I tell them to relax, to let go of their problem, and suggest that it might help if they think of something beautiful – a view – a pet – a beloved child, perhaps. There are some simple verses in David's leaflet that were written especially for this purpose:

When you are receiving healing —
　　Peace, be still – imagine
　　You can hear the sighing trees,
　　– The birdsong from the branches
　　– The murmuring of bees.
　　Peace – be still – and wonder

At the beauty of the rose
As the satin petals open
And their golden heart disclose.
Think of pine-clad mountains
Mirrored in the lake below.
Then – Peace, be still, be tranquil,
And let God's healing flow.

(H.C.V.)

Soft music is always played throughout the healing sessions, and I try to keep voices and laughter down in the waiting room, though it's sometimes difficult! David likes to hear the laughter, anyway, – it means that the patients will come through to him relaxed and receptive to healing.

It is always a great joy to us when, later, a patient says "something is happening to me – apart from the healing – and I want to know what it is". We suggest that the two leaflets should be read again, as they will probably mean much more to the patient now that the *body* is being healed, and the *mind* is being awakened. Soon the *spirit* will begin to stir, love and compassion will begin to flow, and the patient will be whole again. We keep a supply of books for patients to borrow, but we try to fit the book to the need – you cannot feed a new born babe with steak and kidney pudding, and one indigestible morsel may cause the patient to discard the whole meal, so the choice of book is important. Then, of course, they come to the next "Questions and Answers" sessions, and find that they are not alone in their need for knowledge. David is in his element at these meetings, but they are no "ego trip". His message is simple – the healing is from God – and he is unshakeable in that. He has always maintained that he is "a simple sort of chap", and the more wordy questions are reduced, by him, to the basic query, and answered accordingly. As in the healing sessions there is plenty of humour around. These are joyous occasions, a meeting of like-minded folk who are happy to be able to talk freely to David about their doubts and anxieties and to have them openly discussed and eventually dispelled.

Inevitably, some general questions appear at every session, but occasionally we get one that shows that the speaker is seeking a deeper insight into the source of his healing, and the answer sets others thinking, so that the questions thereafter tend to come as a result of that thinking, and the pattern changes.

The following examples make a pretty fair cross-section of questions dealt with at the meetings held in 1984-85:

Q. **Does giving Healing tire you?**

A. No. Just the opposite. It exhilarates me. At the end of the day, when I may have given healing to between 40 and 50 patients I am so elated that I don't want to stop. You must realise that I give nothing. I am purely a channel for Divine Healing. I tap an inexhaustible supply – a constantly filled reservoir – of love and energy, which flows through my hands to the patient.

Q. **What happens to you when you give healing to a new patient?**

A. The patient will normally have told me, briefly, what is wrong, or where the pain is. Depending on the problem, I either go direct to the seat of the pain or place my hand on the back of the neck, where I sense the nervous system. I then become completely detached from, but still aware of, what is happening around me, and in the internal silence the healing begins to flow. I raise and extend my consciousness, and in some way identify with the patient, and the power permeates us both. I will keep my hands in that area until I am aware of a change, a softening, within the patient, and I know that that place has had enough healing. I am now so in tune with the patient that the body tells me where healing is needed, and I know that I must go to a different area, often to the amazement of the patient who demands "How did you know that my foot – or knee – or arm – was sore?" I didn't. Not mentally anyway. Sometimes I return to the site of the original pain but if it is still softened I leave it. Often the patient only tells me of one problem, but the healing force may lead me to three or four, because the pain isn't always where the problem is!

Q. Are you saying that healing pervades the whole body, and can heal even where the patient is unaware of the need?

A. Yes. Healing is for what needs healing, and I can think of several instances where this has happened. I remember one patient who was receiving healing for a troublesome hip and found to the great surprise of herself and her chiropodist, that her bunions had disappeared. I had no idea that she had them – she had never mentioned them to me – nor had my hands been drawn to that particular area. Another lady came for healing for lower back trouble, and a raging toothache went too. "Mind boggling" she called it. Another patient who is in this category has brought a number of problems to me over the years. She usually heals fairly quickly – a swollen knee and ankle yielded almost at once, I remember, but the most interesting thing happened when I was giving her healing for a rather unpleasant sponge-like growth under her big toe-nail, which had been there for some years. I suddenly felt that I should put my hands on her cheeks, and as soon as I did so she felt a tingling sensation in the affected toe, and the problem disappeared. She then remembered that she had had a very difficult tooth-extraction just before the growth on the toe had appeared – whether there was any connection I do not know, but when my hand was on her upper jaw, the toe was healed.

The loveliest thing that happens is when a patient comes for healing for a physical problem, and becomes a more loving and tolerant person as a result. Relatives will sometimes phone and say that someone is so much nicer to live with since receiving healing. Even people who come as drivers or "moral support" are sometimes affected by the atmosphere of caring and love that is engendered here on healing days. It is this atmosphere that enhances the effect of the healing flow and melts away the dis-ease and dis-harmony, even where it was not known to exist, replacing it with happiness and wholeness. I think it is true to say that, whether the patient is aware of it or not, no-one goes away just physically healed – there is always a deeper change. It may take a long time for the leaven to work, but work it will.

Q. **What happens to the patient during healing?**

A. In the majority of cases he, or she, will be conscious of a feeling of peace as soon as healing begins. Sometimes I am told that my hands were warm, or icy cold, or vibrating, often in quick succession. I am completely unaware of this, it is the patient's nervous system reacting to the healing force. I am only conscious of movement within the patient – a sort of swaying movement as pain is moved and alleviated. When this feeling quickens I know that I must stop.

Q. **How do you know if you can help a patient?**

A. If I feel a sort of flowing movement within the patient's body, not as strong as a vibration, and not necessarily at the seat of the pain, as indicated by the patient, then I know healing will take place. If, after three or four visits, there is still no movement, I know that I cannot help at that time. The patient does not truly want to be healed, or is too tense for the healing to flow. This does not happen often, but it has done so.

Q. **What do you do then?**

A. I suggest another healer. Sometimes a patient and a healer are just "wrong" for each other. No-one knows why, they may get on extremely well together, but the healing will not flow. As happened with Una Lyons and Ted Fricker.

Q. **Is anybody ever healed instantly?**

A. Yes, indeed. These cases are rare, but very exciting.

Q. **What happens?**

A. I am aware of an immediate, intense activity under my hands, followed by a melting, flowing sensation as the problem literally dissolves. This is an all-pervading experience, and the patients are shaken and somewhat bewildered at first. Then as they realise that they are completely free of pain, or can walk without limping – or raise an arm that has been locked, that the iron band of tension round the tem-

ples has melted, then they are wonderfully elated, and, as
Helen will tell you, return to the waiting room muttering "I
can't believe it" over and over again. Which is understandable. It is difficult to believe in miracles in this materialistic
age. But they happen. Luke tells us that after Jesus had
healed Jairus's daughter, he "called the twelve together and
gave them authority . . . to cure diseases . . . and they went
through the villages preaching the Gospel and healing
everywhere." The same Divine love that activated them has
poured through the hands of hundreds of healers since
then, and still does.

Q. **Why don't you heal in Church as you are a Spiritual
Healer (and the Church is the centre of Spiritual life
on earth?)**

A. I have not yet been asked to, and whilst I do feel that it
would be wonderful, and very right, to give God's healing in
a consecrated building, I do not see how it could fit into a
Church Service. Each healing is private and personal, and I
need to be attuned to both my patient and my God before
this most potent force can flow through me to the seat of the
problem. Obviously, it would be lovely if I could heal, in
this way, in the peaceful atmosphere of a church, but I must
stress that healing is available, through me, wherever and
whenever it is needed. The setting is the least important
factor.

Q. **What is meant by Absent Healing?**

A. If a patient who has been receiving contact healing is
unable to come to me for some reason and phones to ask for
Absent Healing I ask him to go and sit quietly in a room by
himself, to relax, and to re-live the experience of healing as
he has known it through my hands. I then raise him up in
my consciousness, and he receives healing in the degree to
which he has been able to re-live the experience. Sometimes
this healing is requested by people who have not previously
received it, or on behalf of someone who is unaware of the
request. In these cases, I go into a deep inner silence and in
a state of meditation and prayer, I offer up their names

for healing. I am often asked to do this for people who have gone into hospital for an operation, and inevitably I am told later that they were very calm before and after the ordeal and that recovery was smoother and swifter than usual.

Incidentally, people who have received a great deal of healing do not always need even to contact me for Absent Healing. They can "tune in" to me as though I was a radio receiving set, and by re-living their healing experience, the healing will flow to them without my being aware of it. The more experienced they become the less they need contact healing.

Absent Healing is also very effective when it is sought for animals. Pip, a Labrador, received healing for a skin condition, through his owners' hands, when they "tuned in" to me.

Q. **Could an atheist be a healer?**

A. Obviously, he could not be a Spiritual Healer, but there are many other forms of healing. Reflexology, Acupuncture, Radionics, etc., and he might, presumably, practice those. I really don't know. I imagine that, since an atheist does not believe in God, he does not believe in life after death either, since Christ, the Son of God, appeared on earth after his Crucifixion to prove that very point. That being so, I should not think that an atheist could heal on either the Psychic or Spiritual level.

Q. **Can you help with mental illness?**

A. I have never been asked to. I have helped several people with severe depression and similar conditions, but the amount of help received has always been determined by the build up of drugs in the body. This is sometimes so formidable that healing is almost brought to a standstill.

Q. **Have you ever helped anyone to come off drugs?**

A. Yes. When a television programme highlighted the fact that many people had been taking various type of sleeping pills for years, even though some of them should not have been prescribed for more than a few months, I had several patients who had decided to try to do without them. Some

of these people were in a quite pitiable state, but with deter-
mination and Spiritual help they were able to stop taking the
drugs and to cope with life without that particular
"prop".

Q. **Do you ever feel that a patient is not ready for
healing?**

A. Yes, that has happened. Sometimes I have been able to
alleviate, but not heal a condition. The patient has returned
later with a different problem and the original disease has
then been healed as well. I remember that a small boy was
brought to me with a skin complaint that I was not able to
clear. His mother continued to come, however, and one day
I was prompted to tell her to bring her son back again. This
time healing was complete.

Q. **Could one heal oneself?**

A. I would imagine that this would be possible if, through
meditation, one was able to raise the consciousness and so
renew the life source that has become thin and depleted
through illness. Meditation must help, in any case, by pro-
moting a feeling of peace and tranquility and thus reducing
the fear that aggravates all illness, and is the main cause
of many.

Q. **Is the healing of animals part of your work?**

A. Yes. One of the most rewarding parts. Animals (and
small children) usually respond much more easily and quickly to healing than do adults, which makes nonsense of the
claim that one must have faith for the healing to be effective.
Neither of these groups know anything about faith, yet my
experience is that they are aware of the help they are receiving and accept it naturally. The most mettlesome horse, the
most boisterous dog, the most excitable child all become
quiescent, almost somnolent, under my hands as healing
comes through. I have never been hurt by an animal, or
rejected by a child.

Q. **What do doctors think about your healing?**

A. They are suspicious. I think that their training is so

drug-based and technical that they could not easily recognise or understand the result of healing. One hopes that, one day the B.M.A. will relax its persistent denial of the effectiveness of Spiritual Healing, and that we shall see more doctors coming to us for help. Divine Healing has so much to offer, and it is offered with humility – no healer would deny the wonderful advances in medical sciences and skills in recent years, but sometimes, for some patients, they don't work, and healing does. Could not the two be complementary?

Q. You tell me I must relax. How can I?

A. Tension is the result of dis-harmony in your life, which brings about dis-harmony in your person. It is caused by fear. Fear of illness, of losing your job, of reduction in income, of separation from a loved one – there are a hundred different reasons for the sleeplessness, indigestion, headaches and other symptoms of tension. You can only be released from the imprisonment of tension by relaxation – letting go. Reading, or listening to music, is an excellent way to relax, but when the book or the record/tape is finished, the worries crowd in again. Many people find that Yoga is the path that leads to peace of mind through a combination of physical disciplines and meditation.

And meditation. That is the certain way to lasting relaxation, to peace. And it costs nothing, except time. You don't have to get up to switch anything on, you just have to sit down and switch your thoughts off. Which is not easy, let no one tell you it is. After all it was your racing mind that caused your troubles in the first place, worrying about problems, real and imagined, in the past, present and future, and you can't stop a merry-go-round in a minute.

But try. Go into a room where you can be quiet, and close the door. Sit comfortably, so that you can forget your body, close your eyes, breathe deeply and slowly, and try to shut out all thought. If this is your first attempt at meditation you will find this almost impossible – thoughts will come crowding in. Push them gently away, don't get tense about it, just try to disregard them and return to your pursuit of peace. If it is obvious that you are not going to be able to shut them out, then at least get them under control by deciding what you will think *about.* Calmly choose a theme, and deliberately explore every facet of that theme. What better than the beauty of Nature, there are so many treasures there, flowers, trees, birds, animals, mountains, lakes, jewels. Material for many a meditation.

Suppose you start with a flower, the tiny hearts ease perhaps. Really look at it, visualise that lovely little face, purple and white and gold, the delicate markings, the pretty shape. Slowly inspect it, then go from the flower, through the leaves to the stem, then down to the tiny roots seeking the life-giving force that sustains it. Imagine that force flowing through it, and through everything that grows, and realise that it is the same life-force that is flowing through you. Another time think of a tree, say – a weeping willow, silhouetted against a glowing sunset. Look at the graceful shape of it, then travel up from the tips of the slender arching branches, down through the trunk into the great roots pushing into the earth in search of the life-force pulsating there. And in the earth are the jewels. Imagine you are holding them your hand, and look long and deep into the heart of each one. See the lovely glow of the ruby, the flick of flame in the fire-opal, the cool serenity of the amethyst – the healing stone. These, too are vibrating with the life-force that you are trying to contact in meditation. The Divine Spark, the "Father within", the Infinite Love that pervades and sustains every living thing, that is waiting to take over your life and make the rough places smooth "the crooked place straight" – the Love that will never leave you or forsake you, that wants only your love in return. When you can exclude all thought, so that there is complete silence and stillness, if only for a few moments, then a feeling of peace and serenity will flow in, and you will get up from your meditation knowing that your life will never be the same again, that you are no longer alone, that all will be well.

Things will happen that you would previously have called coincidences. Now you will know they are not.

This will not happen straightaway. If you find that you really cannot still your mind, then give up, and try again later, whenever you can spare a few minutes to be quiet. First thing in the morning, and last thing at night are the best times, but, as you get more adept, you will find yourself snatching a few moments of peace and renewal whenever you need them, when walking alone, or even on a bus! It is not easy – things that are really worth doing seldom are – but do persevere, even though it may take months, even years. The prize is perfect peace.

CHAPTER 6

FOLKINGTON PLACE

About two years before I met David he was introduced to a very lovely and warm-hearted lady, Mrs. Pearl Voorspuy, who lived at Folkington Place, a beautiful old house, situated at the foot of the South Downs. There was a dwelling-place on this site at the time of the Sussex Domesday, and houses have been built, destroyed and re-built there, – often from the original materials, – throughout successive centuries, the present one remaining unchanged since 1813, when a new wing was added. Couched comfortably amidst paddocks, stables, and a very beautiful and unique "chalk garden" this house was to be the setting for many successful and dramatic healings.

At first David gave healing only to Mrs. Voorspuy, her husband Capt. Henk Voorspuy and members of their family, together with their horses and pets. Then gradually, friends joined the healing sessions and the Monday evenings became busier and busier. Some of these friends were farmers, and then David found himself giving healing, and Absent Healing, to a variety of farm animals, including horses, sheep, and Mrs. Moonstone, a beautiful Jersey cow, who thereafter sent him regular gifts of cream in acknowledgement of her return to full health.

Among the farmers who benefited from Spiritual Healing was one who made a rapid recovery from brucellosis, and another, a mushroom grower, who had been involved in a car crash several years earlier, and who still had a trapped nerve in his neck. This had not responded to any treatment, including manipulation under anaesthetic, and he had been told that it would probably get worse as he got older, and might mean the wearing of a permanent support. It was after one such session that he heard about David, and came to see him, wearing a very rigid neck collar. He was disinclined to remove this, knowing that he would be in great pain across his shoulders and down his arms if he did, but David finally persuaded him to take it off – and he was healed. His spine is now fully functional, allowing its owner to carry out all the tasks, including heavily lifting, that are necessary to the running of his business, which nowadays includes the repair and maintenance of all types of farm machinery and vehicles.

Leon, a young relative of the Voorspuys, was born with weak hips – so weak that it was thought that he would never be able to lead a normal life. Doctors thought that an operation, to build up the pelvic area by inserting plates, might be necessary when he was older. He was brought to David four months before he had to see the surgeon about the proposed operation, and was given healing weekly during that period. When the interview and tests took place the verdict was that the pelvic area was now so strong that no treatment of any kind was considered necessary.

Capt. & Mrs. Voorspuy have friends and relatives in many parts of the world, and there is a constant flow of visitors to Folkington. Many of them have received healing through David whilst they have been here, including John, a young farmer from New Zealand, who is engaged to Pearl's niece, Sophia. Shortly before his visit to England in 1984 he had a cartilage removed from his knee. The operation had gone wrong, he was in constant pain, and had little mobility in that joint. David saw him about half-a-dozen times, and the end result was complete freedom from pain and full movement restored to the knee. He is now leading a fully active life on his farm in New Zealand.

Monique was another very active person, a great friend of Pearl's, she had been told by "the top people" (her expression) that she had a crumbling spine and must henceforth lead a completely inactive life. As she was a very keen rider and yachtswoman, and also enjoyed travelling extensively,

this was shattering news indeed. She was somewhat reluctant to come to David, and did not feel any real benefit from
the first healing session so decided not to come again.
However, Pearl persuaded her to do so, and thereafter her
healing was progressively effective. After very few visits she
was again participating fully in all her sporting activities,
and has continued to do so. She has also recently been on
extended visits to America and Australia.

When David gave up his job to devote all his time to healing, Pearl and her husband opened their house and gardens
to strangers as well as friends, and soon there was a steady
stream of patients arriving throughout Monday afternoons
and early evenings. In the summer Pearl loves to see her
visitors strolling through the gardens, admiring the unusual
and beautiful effects achieved by her friend and gardener,
Miss Priscilla Coventry. This quite exceptional lady, now in
her late 70's, copes with all the flowers, shrubs, fruit trees,
vegetable gardens, and extensive greenhouses. Scurrying
along in her russet-coloured smock, she really seems to be
the Spirit of the Garden, with an uncanny ability to vanish
when you want to ask questions that she hasn't time to
answer. Many a time I have been within yards of her, turned
a corner, and she just wasn't there! Quite disconcerting. But
the pictures she creates are breathtaking. Great swatches of
glorious colour, softened by the delicacy of tall, golden
grasses. Tiny, brilliant flowers like jewels, barely an inch
above the brown earth. It is a garden full of heart-stopping
beauty for me. I love it.

Miss Coventry takes healing "exceptionally well" accord-
ing to David. Her back troubles, the occupational disease of
all gardeners, yield quickly to healing, and when she presented David with two swollen hands looking "like
lobsters", complaining that she couldn't work with hands
like that, the pain went as soon as healing commenced, most
of the swelling had gone before the session ended, and the
hands were back to normal within a week. At one time she
had acute pain in the solar plexus, and was told that it was

deterioration due to age and that she must not bend – (difficult not to bend when you're a gardener) – but again the trouble yielded easily, as did a very painful ear condition. Not only was an operation averted this time, but her hearing improved as well!

Sadly, Mrs. Voorspuy herself has not been healed – she has Multiple Sclerosis – but she has been helped (she says immeasurably) to cope with the slow deterioration in her mobility. This most courageous lady now holds court from her wheelchair, and court indeed it is, especially in summer. She has always been a keen and knowledgeable gardener, and, knows the position of every rare and lovely plant in her garden. The peace and beauty of this place must be both a solace and a sadness to her as she propels herself in her chair beside the borders she once tended. A very special relationship has developed between herself and David, one of utter trust and unspoken understanding through the sharing of her pain. But there is no bitterness, no envy, in Pearl. No-one rejoices more when the miracle of healing takes place in her house, especially when a young person, whose life is suddenly overshadowed by a dread disease has that shadow removed, and hope for a full life restored through Spiritual Healing.

Such a one was Rosemary, a brilliant young woman, the only one in a male-orientated world to carry out her particular job. For the past five or six years she had been working extremely hard, sometimes as much as a twelve hour day, and leading a very full social life also, so it was not surprising that, when she went for a check-up before going to America on holiday, she admitted to her G.P. that she had been feeling tired for sometime, and that, yes, the lump in her neck had been there for some months, but she didn't think it was important. The result of that confession was a cancelled holiday and a spell in a nursing home, during which a biopsy was performed. Subsequently, one of her 37th birthday presents was the news that she had Hodgkin's Disease, that she had probably had it for about 2½ years, and that her tiredeness was due to the facts that her glands had not been working properly for sometime. A month of tests, scans, X-Rays (after a dye injection) followed, and she was then put on a full course of radiotherapy. The whole area from waist to ears, back and front was treated every day for several weeks. At the end of that ordeal, feeling, she says "totally lifeless" she met David.

In a wonderful "Thank You" letter she writes "I remember our first meeting well and as I had always found it difficult to admit to being tired or below par I think I even found it difficult to admit this to David who was – as I thought even then – my last hope to achieve anything like normality for a future life. David tells me that when we first met he felt there was almost no life source in me – something which he had experienced only very rarely and mostly in very elderly patients – certainly not with someone aged 37! He also felt that I was totally "charred and burnt out". Luckily he didn't tell me this, but was exceptionally cheerful and said he could help."

Rosemary had been told that she might need chemotherapy as well, but that decision could not be made until the full effect of the radiotherapy was known. There were only a few weeks to go when she met David, but, when she kept the appointment, the scanner was out of order. This gave Spiritual Healing a little more time, and when the test was finally made, chemotherapy was not needed.

In the final paragraph Rosemary writes "I will never be able to thank David enough and I hope that the above account of the past year may be of some help to others. As I write this, having just celebrated my 38th birthday, I count myself very lucky to have had the privilege of meeting David and getting my priorities right, perhaps for the first time, and I hope that I have many years ahead of me when I can use the life that has been given back to me. I think as a closing comment it might be pertinent to tell you what my specialist said when he told me I was in remission – "well, God has spared you for a reason – now go and find out what it is!" In a way I knew that he was going to say this and whilst I acknowledge that the radiotherapy was a great help in killing what was a rampant disease I feel David has made me far more aware of life and my part therein and I hope he knows the energy which he has undoubtedly created within me will be used most sparingly and lovingly to help others where possible. For this I will never be able to thank him adequately." Truly, this was holistic healing.

Following this, it is hopeful to be able to report that the radiologist who treated Rosemary has since sent another patient, Angela, to David. She had a similar medical history, and treatment. After just three healing sessions there was a marked improvement in her general condition and some lumps on her head, which were causing concern, have now disappeared.

Noel, a near neighbour and good friend of the Voorspuys, has a very rare complaint – Scleroderma, with the added complication of osteo-arthritis. When she first came to David her neck was swollen and painful. After the first healing session all pain disappeared and she could move her head freely. The fingers of her left hand were incurved – they are now straight and, she tells me, she is now free of osteo arthritis. The muscles in her arms were rigid when healing began, but they are now responding, slowly but regularly, to this treatment.

Another of Pearl's protegées was Susan, whose neck "seized-up" completely. Her osteopath could not help, so it was decided that she should undergo manipulation under anaesthetic. A friend of hers had recently had such manipulation and received no benefit and Susan was therefore reluctant to agree to the operation. At Pearl's suggestion she came to David, and there was a noticeable improvement after the first healing session. She can now move her head freely, without pain.

During the past seven years practically every member of the Voorspuy family has received healing through David. The eldest son, Rufus, had been troubled by an ulcer which suddenly flared up, just before he was due to fly to S. Africa. His visit was for both business and pleasure – they have many friends out there – and he knew there would be a lot of social drinking involved. He was in great pain when David saw him, but the ulcer began to yield as soon as healing began. David felt it "dissolve" under his hand, so did Rufus, who, after a few minutes was able to prod and pummel the place where he had recently felt so much pain. When he phoned his parents to tell them of his safe arrival in Africa he added "Tell David I've drunk about 14 pints of beer today!" It's very hot in South Africa!

Rufus has received healing many times since then, the most recent problem to yield being a displaced disc near the top of his spine. This was, of course, extremely painful and crippling, but again it moved smoothly back into place under David's hand, leaving just a little soreness, which disappeared at the second healing session.

He owns and trains racehorses and several of these have also benefited from Spiritual Healing. Another horse, Kirsty, belonging to friends of the Voorspuys, was in great distress and pain due to a large open sore on one leg. The leg was very swollen, and as the condition did not respond to treatment, the vet suggested that she might have to be put down. He went away for three weeks and was amazed to find, on his return, that the leg was practically healed. David had been called in meanwhile, and found that Kirsty took healing very well and was soon completely fit. Two years later he was introduced to her foal. She has had no pain or problems since, but the leg is slightly misshapen.

There are always dogs around at Folkington. They tend to be amiable and self-sufficient, going sturdily about their business, and if they are not too happy about the weekly invasion of their territory by David's canine patients, they are far too well-mannered to show it. Zoe, a racing whippet clearly had them puzzled, but they were aloofly kind to her, which was as well for she was very highly strung. She raced very successfully, but would "go to pieces" after the race.

Her back leg seemed to weaken, and she would fall. The problem was in the back of her neck, where swelling and blockage would occur after intense activity. She took healing very well, and the trouble has disappeared.

Two other visiting dogs came from Kirsty's home. One, an elderly miniature dachshund had strokes until healing stopped them, the other, a young golden labrador, had a back injury which caused weakness in his hindquarters, so that he was unable to walk far. The owners suspected that he had been illtreated before they took him, but he responded well to healing and the back is now o.k. He still comes occasionally for treatment on lumps of gristle in his body that are softening and disappearing.

Softening and disappearing. As the tensions, the tight knots of pain, the rigid muscles, soften: – as worries about a small boy's hips, about inability to lead an active life again, about the fate of a favourite horse, disappear; as God's love, appearing as Spiritual Healing, pours itself through a healer's hands in the lovely setting of Folkington Place.

CHAPTER 7

WHAT HAPPENED TO SOME OF
OUR PATIENTS

As I have said I do not ask patients what is wrong with them, so unless they mention their problem or their healing (and most do) they can start and finish their treatment without my being any the wiser. Many send "Thank You" letters, which are kept in a file in my desk, and most people recommend others who phone and say "My friend had her arthritis, or ulcer, or slipped disc, etc. healed, and I have the same trouble, so I am wondering if Mr. Sampson could help me", and then I know why her friend always chose a high, hard chair, or consistently refused a cup of tea!

As I got further into the production of this book, however, I realised that if the message of the Healing Force was to give hope to the greatest number of readers, then I needed to be able to quote a real diversity of case histories. I therefore begged David to search his memory for unusual or spectacular healings that I had missed. He found this difficult, which is understandable – after all, he has given Spiritual healing to hundreds of people already and, I repeat, it is possible to become blasé about miracles! One feels very guilty about this, but when treatment is finished and God has been thanked, then I put an asterisk against the patient's name in the appointment book and move someone off the waiting list.

However, my quiet persistent nagging eventually bore fruit. He would suddenly burst out "Deidre – ask Deidre, she's got an interesting story" or "Bernie – that would make good reading" and so on. So, I asked Deidre, and Bernie and others, and I got my stories, and I hope you agree that they are good reading indeed.

Deidre, poor lass, began "passing out" for no apparent

reason, and was told that there was something wrong with her pituitary gland. A brain scan was arranged for six weeks ahead, and she came for healing in the meantime. At one of those sessions David felt something "dissolve" in Deidre's head, and thereafter there were no more "passings out" and the brain scan showed no enlargement or other irregularity.

Bernie's misery had been of rather longer duration. Nine years ago a specialist diagnosed colitis. He was put on drugs, the initial dose of 8 pills per day increasing over the years to 22 a day, plus Predsol. By this time he was unable to work, was having up to 15 bowel movements in an hour and was literally living in his bedroom, which was next to the bathroom, quite unable to leave the house. He was also on a diet of white bread, without crusts, and water. He was rapidly losing weight. After a while the diet was supplemented by a few ounces of chicken breast, and later 4 ounces of potato, plain boiled, without salt, was added. His dinner on Christmas Day, 1984 was just that, white bread, white chicken, white potato.

Then he heard about David. He was quite sceptical about Spiritual Healing, but desperate enough to try anything. After the first visit the friend who had recommended David asked him if he had "felt anything happening" during healing. Bernie hesitated, then said "Promise you won't laugh". The promise extracted he then continued, "I feel as though I have a block of wood or a slab of concrete, in the seat of my pants". He has had that sensation, in some degree, after each of the eight healing sessions he has now attended. At the second one he told David that what he longed for most was a cup of tea. "Helen's making tea" said David "Try one". No ill effects. Since then he has never looked back. He started eating and drinking whatever he wanted, and when he came for his seventh session he said he'd really "thrown the book" at his stomach that week. He had had Chinese food, and a "pub curry" with a pint of beer. He feels completely fit and comfortable inside, and, to use his own words

"I only see blood when I cut myself".

Robert sustained a perforated eardrum after a car accident, and went to see a leading E.N.T. specialist. As a result he was advised to wait a month to see how much natural healing took place, and then return. The verdict then was that there was still a large hole, which would need surgery, and it was suggested that he enter the Nuffield Hospital the following week. He was very reluctant to do so however, and when a business acquaintance suggested he should come to see David, he cancelled the hospital appointment, and came just once for Spiritual Healing. Sixteen days later the ear was completely healed without any scar tissue at all. He writes "the doctors were rather bemused, to say the least, and my explanation was greeted with "the body is a wonderful thing".

Multiple Sclerosis is a terrible disease. It can strike with such violence that the victim can be in a wheelchair within six weeks of the onset. Sudden blindness can occur, may be lasting only ten minutes, but terrifying. Legs can buckle without warning, arms refuse to carry any weight, conversation stop suddenly as the mind goes completely blank. Pain can be paramount, sleep a scarcity. All this happened to Ann, the good friend who has typed this M.S. for me, and who is now, thanks to Divine Healing, leading a full and happy life, including frequent trips abroad with her husband, on business or holiday.

Some letters that we receive speak only of the physical healing received, but the counselling that accompanies the healing is of equal importance, as the following letter shows:

Dear David,

Suitable words do not tumble easily from my mouth or my pen, but I have wanted so much for you to know that in my heart I feel deeply grateful for the healing and regenerative treatment that both Alec and I have received from you. I bless the day that Alec brought me to your door. I was in a miserable state of pain and depression. Since that time my health has steadily and greatly improved. Although I know that many people are quickly healed, in my case the healing has been gradual. This has been a blessing because during this time, under your gentle influence, I have been able to change negative thought patterns and feelings, the cause of so many of our illnesses, to a more positive state. We have been greatly helped by your own cheerful and optimistic outlook, and especially by your understanding and compassion.

We look forward to seeing you again next Wednesday in the delightful and joyous atmosphere of Helen's little cottage. God bless her and you for the good work you are going for so many of us.

With grateful thanks from us both,

Sincerely,

Helen E.

I shall always remember Catherine's first visit. She sat on the very edge of the chair, her eyes constantly turning to the door, restless and frightened, poised for flight. A victim of both agaraphobia and claustrophobia, and other unnameable fears, she asked anxiously "You won't stop me if I want to leave, will you?" I assured her, gently, that of course I wouldn't, but that I hoped she would stay and see David. She did, but on the next visit, left in panic when another patient started talking about waking up in an oxygen tent in hospital! That was her one and only flight, though, and in a letter to David she says:

Dear David,

As I know that your birthday falls this weekend I am writing to wish you a very happy day.

It seems a good opportunity I think, to express my most heartfelt thanks to you for the great help you have been giving me since I first came to you. I know

I've got a good way to go still, but, after so many years of nervous anxiety and illness I can't tell you how good it is to go out without fear of panic and acute distress. Sometimes, of course, panic will and does strike, but I know now that I can cope with it. This I feel to be the essence of the healing, in my case a gradual strengthening, which will surely in time conquer my habitual apprehensiveness. In the meantine I can assure you that it's a very heady feeling to walk about the town and pop in and out of shops in comfort. On these excursions I sometimes meet someone who has known me well, and invariably he or she will comment with great surprise upon seeing me cheerfully going about – and on my own.

So please accept my most appreciative thanks.

And – a happy birthday to you.

> Sincerely,
>
> Catherine T.

Another agaraphobic had the further complication of Crohns Disease to cope with, but after six weeks was able to report:

"After your healing visit today I thought how incredible it is that six weeks ago you came to see a woman in considerable pain and discomfort, also suffering from agarophobia and unable to do shopping. Today I have no pain and able to go shopping without any fears.

Your perception of people and their problems is remarkable, such is your kindness and understanding. I thank the Almighty that the gift he has given you is being endowed on so many who are suffering either mentally or physically and there is no doubt whatsoever that you have been blessed with a very wonderful and inexplicable gift.

When you are healing a sense of peace and tran

quility always seems to come to me, as does a sense of affinity.

Thank you for the time you have given me and above all, the health you have restored to make me a happier and healthy woman again.

Yours very sincerely,
Olive M.

John was an athletic type – especially keen on tennis, but he sustained an injury to his neck some 25 years ago, which gave him constant pain and restricted head movement. He had various treatments from different specialists, with no long-term improvement. One of John's friends was the mushroom farmer with the neck collar and he suggested a visit to David. Healing was effective, the pain went, and John was able to turn his head, which he had not been able to do for many years. A more recent knee injury also yielded quickly to treatment, so the tennis courts are being pounded by John's feet once more.

Sometimes the stories patients tell of engineering jobs that have been done on them make me wince. I did just that when I read Christine's letter:

> "After three operations on my spine, and eventually having to have a fusion and screws put in the base of the spine, the pain was still unbearable, with my left leg partially numb and noticeably dragging, which made walking at all virtually impossible without sticks or help. Further medical consultations pointed to another stay in hospital with possibly more operations. Still a black outlook. Then I was told about David and how he had helped a friend in a lot of pain.
>
> With a sceptical approach I went and how very glad I did, after only a few sessions I found I was able to stand and walk more upright and stairs were more bearable. I continued for further visits and found I

was able to walk with no pain and no sticks. I feel a new person after several years of unbearable pain and misery. I shall always be eternally grateful to David and his wonderful healing.

Gratefully yours,
Christine T.

Soon after receiving this letter, Christine was sighted riding a bike!

One day recently a patient asked me how the book was getting on, adding "I bet you are only mentioning the spectacular cures, the cancers and so forth, but, you know, the fact that my sinuses are clearing after only a few visits is just as much a miracle to me, after years of discomfort". It must be, I do realise that, and it is the reason why I decided to devote a whole chapter of this book to "case histories", and to make them as varied as possible. Consistently healthy people may find them uninteresting, but I am hoping that every one of them will "speak" to someone who is trying, hopelessly, to "live with" some miserable problem, and that they will be prompted to seek help from Spiritual Healing.

Dale is mentally retarded. He is also very blest. He has a wonderful mother who has helped him make the most of his capabilities by consistently supporting and encouraging him and he has also had from childhood, a great love for his church. His mother says "he often has conversations with the Lord, in fact he taught himself to read from the Bible because he was so determined that he *would* be able to read it."

When he first came to David he was 38, still having to "break-up" words when reading, but he now reads much more fluently. He was also very moody and withdrawn, quite morose at times, and often embarrasingly rude. His behaviour "spoilt friendships". Not now – Dale is now a really happy person, able to mix with other people, to join in many activities, to converse with his mother's friends, to be relaxed and helpful with visitors. Certainly he is a great favourite with our patients when he comes for one of his very infrequent healing sessions. His mother, too, has been greatly helped throughout these five years, she says healing has given her "Peace from within: something I never dared hope to achieve, so you see we have so many reasons for saying Thank you David, and Praise the Lord".

Esme was an elegant lady, always very smartly dressed, and I was therefore, not surprised to hear that she had been a tailoress, and had also loved making toys and silk flowers. Now, however, her sight had been affected by a circulatory problem, and she could not see to thread a needle. A few weeks after her first visit I was planning to hold a sale of toys and other craftwork in aid of funds for the Federation of Spiritual Healers. Esme said she thought she could help, and in due course brought along some lovely *small* furry toys, so much harder to make than the big ones – a couple of soft toys dressed in tiny fairisle jumpers, which must have knited on cocktail sticks, and for me, a spray of exquisite silk roses, which still brighten a corner of my sitting room. She is now dressmaking again, and indulging in her other favourite occupation, fancy cookery.

Her husband, George, had a "lymphatic condition" for some time, but he is not now having any medication, as it has stabilized, and, to quote George's letter "I am sure it can only improve from now on". He goes on to thank David for the help they have both received, and to hope that he will continue the "good work" for many years to come.

One person who is making sure that David continues the "good work" is my "egg-man", a marvellous chap named Joe. He delivers eggs all over the town, cheerfully climbing many flights of stairs to deliver half-a-dozen eggs to some dear old soul, only to find a note saying "no eggs today, thank-you" or, worse still, "Could I have another half dozen, please?" Nothing seems to upset him, he even delivers 3 eggs – or 4 eggs – to some of his elderly customers. He was very interested in Spiritual Healing from the start, and had a theory about it. He was a great one for theories and logical explanations was Joe, rather favouring the "electrical force" idea, which he enlarged on weekly until he hurt his foot and came for healing. This proved to be gentle – no force was felt – but effective, and he now carries a stack of David's leaflets in his van. Any customer who merely mentions an incapacity is promptly given a treatise on Spiritual Healing, and my phone number! He has since told me that his mother was a Spiritualist and had received marvellous healing when he was a child, so he was half-indoctrinated already, when he met "his" healer, and surrendered his "theory" without a struggle.

Taking news of the "good work" even farther afield was Bob, a young man who regularly flew over from Holland for healing. In 1979 he learned that he had Ankylosing Spondylitis, that it was incurable, but that drugs would reduce the pain. They didn't. On a visit to England he met David, received immediate relief from pain, followed by a steady loss of rigidity as healing sessions continued, and now writes that "it gives me no bother at all". He came to see us recently, and announced that he now plays Rugby.

Looking back over this chapter I see that it has included a pituitary, long-term colitis, a perforated eardrum, internal pain and acute depression, Multiple Sclerosis, Agaraphobia and Claustrophobia, Crohns Disease, a fused spine with screws in it, a non-turnable head, Sinus trouble, Mental Retardation, loss of sight and a lympathic condition. To those I would add a frozen shoulder, whose owner wrote to thank David "for the miracle you have performed on my body and mind. You will say, I know, that it wasn't you, but you directed the power on to me . . . should worse befall me I shall fly to you for help in secure knowledge of receiving it". Also an ulcerated leg that had been treated for 14 months, but made no progress, but, to quote again "shortly after my one visit to you my ulcer healed up completely and I have had no trouble with it since". A fair cross-section of complaints, I'm sure you will agree.

But this book began with my friend Ella, and I think it will round this section off very nicely if I include the letter David received after a visit she made last year. She had phoned from Cleveland to say that she was in great pain and distress and would like to see David. After staying three days with me and receiving three sessions of healing through David this is what she wrote:

Dear David,

It was well worth every yard of the 600 miles round trip to visit you last week!
Words are very inadequate to express our deeper feelings, but I must write to thank you for the healing of my alarming head pain, and, for the rich spiritual blessing which you gave.

It was such a joy to be with Helen again too, and as you so rightly say, the process of healing starts with her influence. Her home radiates peace, with happiness and laughter, and we all feel relaxed, such aid to our receptiveness of your healing gifts. You did me a power of good between you, and I still feel fine.

As I meditate at home here for continued healing I hear the soft background music which I found so soothing and helpful.

May your radiant happiness and abundance of life force continue to give out that warm glow, re-charging run-down batteries and sick organs, and benefit all who find you and come to you for help. You have an amazing amount of love for all, which I suppose is the greatest healing factor of any.

Carry on your great work, and God bless you,

Ella.

CHAPTER 8

AND TO ME

This account of what happened to just a few of the thousands of people who have received Spiritual Healing in my home during the past five years is now ending, but the effect of those healings is still being felt. Each one was like a stone thrown into a pond, and the resultant ripples are still spreading, carrying the message that Spiritual Healing is available to all who seek it, that it works, and that it can bring physical health, mental peace and spiritual awareness to all who will open their minds to receive it.

And to me? What has healing brought to me – in these five years – on those three levels? Physically I am now very fit. When I met David I was nearly 66 years old, with a permanent backache and an awkward hip joint. I also had a slight spinal curvature, for which I'd had regular massage when I was a child. I am now nearly 72, with none of those disadvantages – nor can I remember having anything wrong with me, except one cold, throughout those intervening years, this in spite of a fairly regular supply of 'flu, tummy and other bugs brought in by patients.

So much for the body, what of the mind?

Well, I tried to keep the Vinall mind very active indeed in 1979, tried, in fact, to fill every moment of every day with some activity, to ensure that I had no time to feel alone, no time to sit and look ahead at the desolate years of widowhood, no time to give way to self pity. Thousands of women, I am sure, would know just what I mean. So, during the previous two years I had gone back to producing amateur drama with two groups, writing the occasional sketch or short play for them, starting a discussion group, and going to classes in various crafts. Then, in 1980 I became President of a large and lively W.I, thereby taking on a wide variety of interests and responsibilities. I went to bed late, with my mind still racing, and woke early with it full of plans. A veritable maelstrom. Then, as healing took over more of David's life, and his patients took over more of mine, I found myself gradually losing interest in these activities so that, one by one, I dropped them. Not without some backward glances, for I had been involved in amateur drama since I was in my teens and had been a founder member, nearly 30 years ago, of the W.I. of which I was now President. Indeed, the warm friendship and unobtrusive help that I received from both groups at the time of my bereavement had helped tremendously in getting me back into the mainstream of life after being housebound, with an invalid husband, for two years. I value greatly the ties of friendship that I still have with them.

And now? I suppose it does take a modicum of mental dexterity, and a large eraser, to fit more than 100 patients, ranging from Artists, Antique Dealers, and Anthroposophists through to Writers, Welfare Workers and Waiters (Portuguese, with large and loving families who all came along as moral support) into about 20 hours of healing time. So, mentally, still ticking over. But calmly now, no panic, no fear of the future, no racing mind, no maelstrom. Just lovely, lasting, peace. Which brings me to the third level.

Spiritual Awareness. The most wonderful of all the gifts that healing brings to those who truly wish to be whole again, to be at-one with the Source of the healing, the Spirit that dwells within each one of us, whatever our skin-colour, status, or religion. Once this awareness is achieved it is the "Open Sesame" to a life so full of love, warmth, happiness and confidence that all worries about money, health, position, family relationships and the other myriad woes that beset us become insignificant and disappear. Starved of attention, they die. But full awareness is not easily achieved, indeed it can take years to acquire perfect peace, complete confidence. One thing, however, is certain. Once you have

experienced that first tenuous flicker, that first will o' the
wisp of wonder at your healing – that is the beginning of
Spiritual awareness. Life can never be the same again. You
are on your way, however hesitantly, to a fuller, happier and
more rewarding way of life.

The speed of your progress depends on you. Some
patients find it easy to accept David's statement that he
"gives nothing". To them Divine Healing is simply another
proof of God's love for them, a belief that is as natural to
them as breathing. They are the lucky ones, their faith – no,
it is more than that – their certain knowledge – is firm
ground under their feet and a stout staff in the hand as they
tread the path to the heights.

For many of us, however, it is not so easy, especially if we
have been taught, as I was, to question everything, to accept
nothing on trust. Even David, who had the benefit of a
happy childhood in a truly Christian home, spent many
sleepless nights, tussling with the problem of where the
healing came from, before accepting wholeheartedly Ted
Fricker's simple statement that it came from God. For me,
with a very insecure and often desperately unhappy
childhood as a base, and a highly critical mind as a further
disadvantage, it was very difficult, at first, not to question
the Spiritual Source of this healing. I kept turning the
evidence this way and that, looking for the joins.

But there weren't any – no human explanation of the fact
that hands that were warm when warmth was needed on
aching muscles could, within seconds, be icy cold near a
twitching nerve, that internal inflammation could "dissolve" under hands through which no visible solvent
flowed, that a definite jolt could be felt through hands lying
gently on shoulders, not connected to any obvious source of
power. That, moreover, the owner of those hands was
unaware of the temperature changes, the vibrations, the
jolts, experienced by those patients. But they were being
healed, and so was I, and soon my mind accepted that this
gift must be of God – and felt a "rightness" in that accep-

tance, as of a latent knowledge justified. This was the first stirring, the first quivering of the antennae, the beginning of Spiritual awareness, but I sometimes wonder if I would have got much further along the Spiritual path had I only received healing, and not thereafter been privileged to work with David.

I doubt it. The leaven of Divine Love had been planted in a mind that was full of Spiritual muddle and uncertainty at that time, and yeast will not "work" in a fridge. I was only certain of one thing, the existence of God. I had only to look at my tiny garden and the hills beyond it to prove that. Like most of my generation I had been sent regularly to Church and Sunday School as a child, and pretty dreary I found it, though it would have been considered near – blasphemy to say so. I was persuaded to continue my attendance into my teens, becoming a Sunday School teacher (because I liked children) and a Guider (because I thought the Guide Law and Promise was a sensible framework for youngsters to build their characters on). But I got no spiritual satisfaction – nothing – from my Church unless it was empty. Then I was aware of God's presence, and was uplifted, – and felt guilty for being so. There was much more emphasis on Punishment for Sin than there was on Redeeming Love in those days, I remember, and I stopped going. I think many young people were driven from the church through being driven to it as children, but I still felt guilty.

Then I reasoned that Christ never said "Come to church" – he said "Come to me", and he was usually to be found on a hillside or by a lake, and that is where I have always felt closest to God. It must have been so simple, so wonderful, to the hundreds of people who gathered to hear it, that message of God's eternal love for his creation, his promise that He would be with them always, that everything he had was theirs, as co-heirs with Christ, his beloved Son. Somewhere in the intervening centuries the glory of that promise has got lost, together with the simple price that must be paid for those blessings, that "Thou shalt love the Lord thy God

with all thy heart . . . and thy neighbour as thyself." Thy
neighbour being everyone with whom you come in contact,
not just the folk next door. The Christian symbol is a fish,
but I think it has become like a stickleback, so many bits of
ritual, and pettiness and divisive religious labels have got
stuck all over it that the original lovely, simple shape has
been obliterated. It is the labels that worry me most, they
have been responsible for so much torture and bloodshed,
in the name of the God who asks for, and promises, only
love! (Happily, there are now many signs of a breaking
down of the barriers between some religions – many
churches now open their doors to people of other faiths,
and in this context it was heartening to see the Greek word
Oikoumene, from which ecumenic is derived, embroidered
on the altar cloth in the nave of York Minister, where com-
bined services of many denominations are often held).

I began to read everything I could find about the other
great religions of the world, especially of India, and began
to feel that here was something that could help me. The
lovely teaching of Gautama fascinated me, and the
Bhagavad-Gita underlined the same theme of love to all. I
was struck by the many similarities with Christian ideals,
and it was then that the idea of "one-ness" entered my head,
and stayed there for many years until the time was right for
me to find the path to the knowledge I had been
seeking.

Meanwhile I married and had two children, sent them to
Church and Sunday School, enrolled one in the Scouts, and
the other in the Guides, and didn't have a lot of time for
intensive reading. I tried to live by the Law, finding the
second part easier than the first because I have always liked
people, from children upwards, loved animals and all other
creatures, and found that beautiful scenery, glorious
sunsets and exquisite flowers have the power to stop me in
my tracks. Not difficult to love *them*, but I was still muddled
about God. I suppose I still had this concept of Him as a sort
of Celestial Overseer, somewhere "Up there", keeping a

tally on my good and bad deeds, taking a couple of marks off my score when I told a lie, and putting 'em back when I put some coins in a collecting box. Admirable but not loveable. I still felt unworthy and guilty in a full church, uplifted and at peace in an empty one.

So that's how it was, when I was healed through David. Liking people – I'd had plenty of practice, having worked for eleven years in a London Office with a staff of 4,000, and for twenty five years as a School Secretary – and quite capable of running my own life, thank you. But knowing, in my inmost being that my self-sufficiency was a very thin film in front of a very black void. And that word "one-ness" was still nagging at the back of my brain. I have read recently that, when the pupil is ready, the teacher or the book will appear. And they did. The teacher was Joel Goldsmith, and the book was his "Art of Meditation". David brought it to me and I read it with mounting excitement as I realised that this man had put into words what I had known – without knowing that I knew it – all my life. Here was the theme of one-ness – of a God that permeates everything, a Spirit that flows through every blade of grass, every tree, every creature, everybody, the Infinite Invisible. NOT UP THERE, remotely book-keeping against the Day of Judgement, but DOWN HERE, within everyone of us "closer than breathing, nearer than hands and feet". And loving us, knowing our needs before we know them ourselves, wanting only to make the life He gave us happy, healthy, carefree, perfect. If only we will let Him.

And there's the rub. It's not easy to hand over your life completely when you have always been a fairly competent and efficient sort of person, used to coping with problems on your own. I found it very difficult indeed to "give no thought to the morrow", to stop planning and arranging things in what I was sure must be the right way, and to become a bystander, watching my life being used so wonderfully, so cleverly, to help David prove the existence of a caring God. I used to fume and say "You made me like this –

you gave me this questioning mind. I can't just give everything over – it's too much to ask". Then back I would go to Joel Goldsmith and inevitably open his book at the page with the appropriate answer. Then the peace would come, and I would know that what I was gaining was immeasurably more precious than whatever I was losing. It seemed to me that this man had distilled the essence from all the great religions, from Eastern mysticism and Western Christianity, and presented his simple, powerful message in a way that could be understood and assimilated by most people.

I read as many of his books as I could get hold of, and other modern mystics too. Everyone contributed more pieces to the jigsaw of my knowledge, or underpinned what had been a rather shaky relief, bringing enrichment and radiance to my new-found truth. So many great people, I found, have been worried by the divisive labels. Gandhi, for instance, was in despair because people persisted in believing that there were different gods for Hindus, Muslims and Sikhs. He tried to explain that no religion was superior to any other and that he himself was a good Hindu, Muslim, Christian, Buddhist and Parsi. That surely, is how it should be. There is but one God, and He is Love, and all roads lead to Him.

My own road started with a stiffened wrist and the healing of it. Then the gratitude for that healing led to the questioning of the source of that healing. And to the answer. "It is from God". A simple statement that was to echo through my little house so many times, and to be the first stepping stone on the path to Spiritual awareness for myself and many others. This path, once found, leads through shadowed valleys to shining mountain tops. Dark patches of doubt and uncertainty have to be tramped through before we can ascend to the heights on winged feet, only to descend again into the greyness of lost confidence, wondering whether we ever experienced that radiance. But we did, and we must build on those luminous memories until, almost imperceptibly, the valleys grow smaller and the hilltops are plateaux, through our every-growing awareness of the loving Presence in and around us. The Presence that, I know, puts the right thoughts in my mind, the right words in my mouth when they are needed by someone desperate for comfort and understanding.

When I started this book the first part, describing how it all started and what joy and love poured through my house on Healing Days, just flowed from my pen, but when I wanted to write this last chapter, I just couldn't! I have been writing long enough to know the many facets of "Writers Block" and most of the tricks to defeat it, but this was different. For three months nothing came at all. I could not write. But I read, how I read, and gradually the multiplicity of mind-knowledge went down and became the simplicity of heart-knowledge – "the longest journey" – and I could write again. Could write again, with humility and gratitude, of the many blessings that followed that first great gift – the friendship of David Sampson. A friendship that warmed and gave purpose to a life that was without aim or direction. It was through his healing hands that I became certain of the existence of God, it was through his discovery of Joel Goldsmith that we both found *where* He existed. We started our Spiritual journey together, but David is way ahead of me now, a constant support when I stumble, and unshakeable rock when I doubt. My very dear friend. Small wonder that I thank God daily that, five happy years ago, I was asked if I could find "a room for David".

CHAPTER 9

AND TO DAVID

Helen has asked me to round off her book with my own comments on my development, as a healer, over the last five years, but since I have always been able to communicate more easily with the spoken rather than the written word, I face the task of writing down my thoughts witg great trepidation. Those who look for any literary merit will seek in vain, but I hope that those who read on might find something of interest from one who has experienced healing "both ways"; and if anything I say helps a better understanding of this most remarkable activity, then I bow willingly to the task.

As I look back over the years, I see several pointers (unrecognised at the time) which quite certainly steered me in the direction that my life was to take. The family that I was fortunate to be born into gave me the security of a united Christian home and many of the probing questions of a youngster of ten years who has experienced 'a something' spiritually, were able to be answered, or at least explored and encouraged. I well recall the joy in my mother's face when I announced that I had decided to become a Minister and I know she would have been happy beyond belief if my later life had followed that course. I am so grateful that before she passed on a few years ago, she was able to rejoice with me in the work that it was my destiny to pursue. However, other interests were to influence me in different directions and at the age of 21, I left my native South Africa and all my family, to visit Britain. I hoped that this might be a working, as well as an educational, visit – that it might even last a year or two, but straight away I felt an affinity with this country and have remained ever since, an ardent fan and supporter of my adopted country.

But it was the spiritual healing which I received at the hands of Ted Fricker that was to be the greatest cause of a change of events in my life, although at the time I could never possibly have imagined to what extent. From the very first occasion that he administered healing, I knew that an amazing change was happening and deep within I was constantly questioning what I was feeling. The physical changes were as obvious to me as they were to those around me. The inner questioning was disturbing and exciting. If this act of healing had (by its very definition) sought and affected a change in me spiritually with a resultant physical betterment, then would that not apply to all – or nearly all – of mankind's illnesses? I could not think of any particular illnesses of mine that were clearly a "punishment" for past sins. There seemed to be many who were rather more expert at every sort of sin and yet were wonderfully well and healthy. And always, I had never lost the wonder of the experience I had had as a youngster, when I felt The Presence. I was pretty certain that that had been a very personal event and one which not everybody was fortunate enough to have had.

Therefore the significance of the spiritual dimension of healing had to be understood. It seemed so simple, that a man – clearly a most unusual and gifted man, but nevertheless a very 'ordinary' man – could bring about such incredible changes against all medical understanding. If he was able to do this just for one needy person it would be quite amazing, but to learn of the many who were healed (and quite a few were personally known to me and so I saw the "before and after") then why was not this the most talked about, written about, matter of this age? Of course, I read the book written about Mr. Fricker and there had been several newspaper articles, but even so, this quite newsworthy activity of healing seemed to be unknown except by those who knew Mr. Fricker and came for healing. Not that he was alone in this work. There were several others that I had heard about, of which Mr. Harry Edwards was probably the most well known. He, (Harry Edwards) drew large crowds to his meetings and his public demonstrations of healing have been well documented and are remarkable. But again, there seemed to be so little real understanding of what was behind these events and only the facts of the physical improvements ever managed to be reported. And yet surely, many like me must have felt in awe of the way in which these men were being used.

Society appears to demand of its doctors a position that they cannot fully satisfy. Of course, the ability of certain drugs to suppress symptoms and pain is not only a great blessing but must be available for our needs. And so very many advances in medicine are clearly of great benefit to us all – but let us just think a while about the use of certain drugs in the light of some knowledge gained through spiritual healing. If a change occurs as a result of spiritual healing that restored health and renders unnecessary the use of drugs to alleviate that complaint, then clearly the original use of that preparation was not the best treatment for that particular problem or patient. It follows surely, that if the use of medicine intended to restore health is successful, then the condition must have been largely physical and an entirely satisfactory conclusion would have been reached. But what if that does not occur, and what if every effort by doctors, specialists and in fact all treatments directed at changing the physical complaint are of no avail? Could it be that until the problem is relieved at source (spiritually) the physical condition will resist? That is what happened to me and has happened to many others.

I started to read any book that offered knowledge on the subject of healing. I found a great deal of information that did not satisfy me and yet I must have been sifting the facts all the time because I was starting to understand a little, just the tiniest little bit, of the mystery of healing by the laying-on of hand. I had the advantage of feeling the effect and of seeing the results in me and in others. And so I was drawn to Ted Fricker, and took every possible opportunity to meet him. I needed to know what motivated him. I had to understand, if I could, what deep connection he must have with the Source of power that could be channelled into such a wonderful work.

Apart from my visits to him for healing, I used to take others there quite often – friends and strangers that I had felt compelled to talk to about the help available at Fricker's Healing Centre – and that gave me further occasions to observe. A friendship developed with Mr. and Mrs. Fricker and their daughter Theresa (who was his receptionist) and I felt so very privileged to call them friends.

My first appointment had been made by a colleague at my office, Jean Johnston, who had been greatly helped with an appallingly painful back of many years duration. Several others in our office had also become patients of Ted Fricker and it was not uncommon for discussions about healing to take precedence over business matters. In fact we became quite a centre of information on healing and were able to help many receive Ted's healing.

And then nine years later at a dinner party to say farewell because my family and I were leaving London to live at Bexhill-on-Sea, he told me that I had the gift of healing. It was explosive information. I had no idea and at once questioned what he had said. He told me that when we first met he knew I had the gift (deeply hidden) and that one day he would know when to tell me – and that was now! This was so incredible that I really could not accept it. My mind raced through many of the marvels I had witnessed over the years. It could not be, I felt, that I, who had had no inclination to heal and not the slightest indication that the possibility existed for me, should have this open to me. Had it not been told to me by Ted Fricker, who had proved his ability to sense a latent gift of healing in others, then I would have discounted it at once. And on reflection, had he told me this before that time, I am pretty certain that it would not have registered. I was not ready until that time.

And so started the most wonderful ten years of my life. At first, the most puzzling, uncertain, hesitant steps of one who could but marvel at the occasional changes that seemed to come about after the laying-on of hands. I continued to study, to try to understand what was happening inside me at a deeper level. Looking at the lives of other spiritual healers, I noted that they were invariably psychic; I was not. In fact, I not only knew very little about the subject, but I did not feel anything either. I expected to sense at least a sort of flow of power (such as I had received in healing) but that was not so. Yet those to whom I administered healing were clearly benefiting. It was obvious from what patients were saying, that they believed I knew instinctively about their aches and pains and where to place my hands. They had a confidence in me that I would have loved to enjoy, but at least it did give me the desire to continue; and so I worked as the manager of a motor business during office hours, and afterwards until about 10.00 p.m. on several evenings a week, as a healer.

By now I was starting to "feel". Sometimes there was an awareness of movement deep inside at places where I had placed my right hand. A sort of sympathetic feeling developed where the patient complained of pain and I was becoming more confident generally in tuning in to them. Always and in every way I tried to understand and to seek knowledge of this gift that by this time had become such an important part of my life – both for me and my family.

I was advised by an established healer to contact a certain Medium, and over a period of about 18 months visited him more or less monthly. He was most helpful. I found him to be a man with the highest Christian principles and much of what he told me was tape-recorded, and it is lovely. But my thirst for true knowledge was unsatisfied, and so I continued to be led, as I felt it, into whatever forms of learning came my way. And by looking at everything with an open mind, but with spiritual discrimination as my guide, I progressed, slowly, towards the objective of understanding the purpose of my life and calling.

One day my wife brought home another book from the local library for me to read – knowing of my pursuit of matters spiritual. It was 'The Art of Meditation' by Joel Goldsmith; and I knew I had found my teacher. The spirituality of this man just came out to me and it is true to say that I devoured the pages as though I was starving. I am a slow reader, and much of it needed to be read many times to "get inside" but I shall always recall the elation that I knew in studying that book.

By this time I had met Helen Vinall and we had become friends. Her home became a place to meet patients, and her ever open door and great warmth of welcome to all who came soon ensured a growing list of those seeking help. We soon realised that our thinking on deeper matters followed similar lines and so developed a bond founded on our mutual understanding and growth. And so it was natural that I should take the library copy of 'The Art of Meditation' for her to read. I say no more than that it was only a few hours later than she telephoned, full of excitement at the book. Joel Goldsmith had clearly made a great impact on her also, and that, for both of us and for many others, has continued. We must have studied twenty or more of his books and his ability to go straight to the centre of all that affects our lives and so to lead on to the ultimate experience of reality is as alive for us as ever it was.

Working during the day and administering healing in the evenings – or at any rate three or four evenings a week – was becoming difficult. Obviously I was hardly good company for my wife and son and as more and more people wanted to meet me, my time at home suffered. Also I was feeling increasingly dissatisfied with a situation which needed me to be very material for nine hours a day and then switch over to a higher spiritual level so that I could become a channel for healing for the next four hours. The thoughts of one constantly impinged on the other as both my business and healing commitments increased. The way seemed to me to be clear. I must give up all interests in business and in earning my living and go into healing full-time. My wife, always so supportive of my healing work, was most understanding, although I think she often had cause to wonder when at first we lived on our savings. I needed time to study and to grow, and to feel that I could give myself to my calling completely and without reser vations. I had to see if this gift of healing would mature if left to grow naturally and without pressure. Anyway, I believed completely that the Divine Source of the healing which flowed through me would provide for my material needs, and so we put 'all our eggs in one basket'.

From the early days of becoming interested in meta-physics, I realised that meditation was imperative to any who would follow a spiritual path. The subject was difficult to understand but I had no idea how very difficult I would find its practice. In time, as I gained a degree of inner peace, I knew that this subject was to become the very foundation of my life and work. The attainment of "the peace that passes all understanding" came with a certainty of one-ness with the presence of God. In that wondrous quietness I find all I need: it is totally fulfilling. It is that state of consciouness that I seek during the laying-on of hands, and in that consciousness of The Presence does the healing take place. I need often to meditate, to continually seek to establish a close link with the Creator. I know that that life force which originates and is sustained from the Creator, is channelled through me when my consciousness is raised during healing. This life force, this loving power which flows, needs a clear clean path and only by constantly practising contemplative meditation am I able to play my part. The times that I spend in meditation and prayer are refreshing, illuminating, often instructive and always rewarding. These words are so inadequate – how can I speak of the sensations, the thrill of attaining, at least in some measure, the very presence of God? It is a state of adoration of God through Christ. It is Christ consciousness.

Absent healing (or distant healing as it is sometimes called) is possible when the mind of the healer is raised, but it is in the quietness, the absolute silence, that this form of healing is most effective, and in meditation that state is achieved. Always there is that deep longing for communion that is satis-fied in the stillness of heart and mind. The letting go of all thoughts and entering into the nothingness of silent prayer.

Prayer, which like meditation is aimed at communication, or more perfectly, communion with God is often disappointing because we do not pray aright. Jesus said (Matthew 6 v 6). When you pray, go away by yourself, all alone, and shut the door behind you and pray to your Father secretly. Joel Goldsmith says commune with the Father Silently, Secretly, Sacredly. Is not the stillness of the mind the lynchpin of prayer? Is it not clear that it is in the silence of the mind that communion with God occurs? A mind busy is not a mind that hears.

Nearly all my life I have had difficulty with prayer. The understanding that God is all knowing and all-loving has seemed to be contradicted by the act of prayer, which itself has been taught to be the means by which we inform the Deity of what is needed. It is conflicting in the sense that what I may at the moment decide is good for me, may not be so in the long term; and even if it is, might it not be bad for somebody else? So why should I believe that God will act in accordance with my wishes at the expense of others? And all this assumes that there is a God figure awaiting requests on where and to whom to bestow His goodness – or more truthfully, the world's good things.

Prayer, rightly used, is something quite different. It is a state of mind in which the one who prays seeks contact with the Divine Source, and is able to become utterly humble, to *know* what is meant by "I can of myself do nothing". That means *no thing*. It means emptying our minds and releasing our attachments. To be able earnestly to seek forgiveness but to ask for that only after there is forgiveness in your heart for all men. To acknowledge that life is lived each minute by God's grace and that therefore we exist absolutely within His power. To see that in His presence there is no disharmony, unhappiness, fear or illness and to therefore seek for that presence only. In prayer, to love God, and to love all others, is to pray aright. No need to ask for protection, for guidance, for health – these exist eternally in the presence of God.

It is good to see that there is a much wider acceptance

generally, of healing. It is certainly on the increase and will greatly benefit all who avail themselves of it. The evidence is overwhelming and well documented and I find in more and more of the patients that have been helped through healing, a readiness to tell their doctors. I pray that the medical profession and much of the Church will look at the Ministry of Healing, in and out of the Church, in a new light and will understand that those who are so very privileged to be part of it, are mostly sincere, compassionate and humble people who have been gifted. To be able to relieve pain and distress and not to feel that that is acceptable to those who should be most concerned – doctors and Church leaders is extremely sad. Several years ago I was granted the status of Healer Member with the National Federation of Spiritual Healers. That body is most active in trying to bring together the doctors and scientists to monitor selected cases for healing so that the whole matter can be better evaluated. That must be exciting news for all healers.

For me personally, I hope that I shall continue in my work for many years yet. There appears to be so much activity surrounding our healing days at Helen Vinall's little cottage, and yet I seem to do so little – usually it is like standing aside and watching a procession of people passing by. The heavy burden of arranging the appointments to suit everybody, often organising lifts for those that need help, suggesting suitable reading matter for any who are becoming interested (we have a little library), offering tea and biscuits and being a constant source of joy to all, is Helen's role. Her life is dedicated to serving any who come to us, and to helping all others in every way she can – but always unobtrusively. She is a tower of strength to me, and I thank God daily for bringing her into this work.

And so at the end of it all, I find myself being certain only of God's love and of wonder at the work that He requires of me – work that I, of myself, do not do but in which I am a channel for His loving kindness to all.